David Lampe
Nov. '86

2-

GRAVES REGISTR

Frontispiece

the vision of this gate:

       granite, stained
         by birds—

Lion's Gate

   which, finally,
   is the stone lion's own
   open mouth, roaring

—is what we pass through

   a taste, a feel:
   the tongue, flame red

—is what passes by

       fangs,
       glistening:

       yellow eyes
       that watch

—is an entry, a sort
   of gate, passage to, exit
   away, the angry maw
   roaring

GRAVES REGISTRY

and other poems

by Keith Wilson

Grove Press, Inc. New York

to Heloise

Contents

Acknowledgments

Some of these poems have appeared in the following magazines: *Ahora, Camels Coming, Camel's Hump, Colorado State Review, Confrontations, Descant, Desert Review, Detroit Artists Workshop Benefit, El Corno Emplumado, Floating Bear, From A Window, Intransit, Magdalene Syndrome Gazette, Ninth Circle, Open Letter, Potpourri, Symptom, Weed, Wild Dog.*

Three poems from "Graves Registry" ("Korea, 1952," "The Singer," and "The Circle") as well as "Note to a Sister" and "Classes" first appeared in *Poetry*. The poems "blood-totem," "Old Love," "The Singer," and "The Hanging of Billy Budd" appeared in *31 New American Poets,* ed. Ron Schreiber (Copyright © 1969 by Hill and Wang, Inc.).

Echoes, Seafalls for Heloise

1

graceful birds, tall yet distant ships
with lateen sails blazing white, sailing
outward before rays of setting gunfire, far
battles: it is they I speak of, touch here.

A woman, newborn, beckons from the waves,
beckons, Lady, from the foam, breasts like suns,
watergleaming emeralds in her hair: it is she
I speak of, turning her voice towards spray,
shining in, tideborne.

2

                         my darling
no bird of the sea touches more gently
than you; far away, the lanterns of war
ships hulled down twinkle, sea winds crying
my name, as you do, racing, long legs flying
through our yard—laughing, your yellow hair
a battle pennant before the sun, streaming ...

             victory over sea
coming later as love, a home safe from waves; challenge,
is a singing in the wind, a crashing

Day of the Wolf

The other ranchers came this morning,
early; in the crisp blue air of Fall
they stood stiffly—each holding his reins
his restless horse, took coffee, nodding
a "thank-you-mam," his rifle hanging
beside him in a scratched leather
scabbard.

        —the wolf was back, three calves
slaughtered yesterday, their white faces flat
on the ground, big eyes splattered with dirt

: Wolf, running free past the traps in search
of fresh meat, he couldn't be fooled by bait.

That evening we got him just the same,
shot him down when he came to smell
the bitch coyote we'd staked out,
got him, horses in a circle he
couldn't cross, but he fought well,
stood his ground, slugs slapping
him down, him getting up, snarling
showing his teeth until he died.

The horses wouldn't carry his hide
back and we left it there, bloody in the
dusk, his skinny body white as a child's
in the waving tall grass.

Classes

they should be held in the open.
free. you should talk, then I:
we will have communion, here under
the bright green leaves of a Spring
all will remember as our awakening.
class, I'm talking to you.
it's important we touch each other,
no matter how foolish the gesture
(this connection, couldn't matter less—
who but a fool cares about commas?
                    I am here,
you, there. ah, but you sleep.
& I drowse. at least we share
this room, let that be recorded:
together, we dream these hours
and, perhaps, each other.
class. I hear your names
like strokes against ancient cymbals,
ghosts, voices answering to a role.
class. we are dying, do you know
that? mustn't we speak, now? or
for God's sake let's end this farce,
let tree roots claim us, spreading
its branches to the sky, let us live
that way, if we can manage no other.

Old Love

Coming down
I, on
Bright Angel

trail, below Kaibab, the long
turning into history and back
towards rock: I suddenly see you,
gone all these years, inset
a fossil leaf, trapped before time,
it is an echo of yourself that sings
the sad notes, these dry notes. Sweet
Gone Canary, turned to dust puffs
caught by the wind racing across blue
canyons, wherever you are, gone blue
and rose, against sandstone or falling
neon across the low clouds, too large
a part of me gets lost in this coming down.

Koyemsi

Those mudheads. Dancing
clowns, born of brother
& sister mating. Eaters
of feces.

Splayed feet. Mud
between the toes, clay
masks & bodies

—humor, insanity
   remain, in them,
   sacred

& these gods are not
under masks, watch
out of the wind
rain growing corn.

Children, children
with pollen in their mouths
laughing, please them,
koyemsi, risen from earth
they who led the People
from the Underworld, risen
from deep clay, the singing

shines in their victory, rite
a celebration of horrors conquered
by dancing feet & laughter, mica
particles flashing out of clay
the laughter comes, dancing.

To My Daughters

Children, walking or playing in the sun or
bright behind low clouds; children dancing
out old rituals all but they forget:

> Lady O, Lady
> O turn around;
>
> Lady O, Lady
> O, touch the
>
> ground, O my
> darlings

skipping to the circling arc of ropes, the
brightness can be lost, daughters who make a man's
house a place of singing—daughters skipping &
out, too, is a way of breaking free before sun.

The Homestead: Carpenter's House

—Fort Sumner, New Mexico

a green frame house trimmed
in white, falling down.

a memory of icetea
served frosted in tall glasses,
of coaloil lamps yellow through
old glass windows

—crickets, wind
in the cedars, New
Mexico in the 30's
where people lived
for evening & our
old men sat smoking
an hour away

—the darkness. Billy
the Kid's ghost walking
the long road from Pete
Maxwell's house to the Military
Cemetery, alone,
his slender gun with its
birdshead grip, his
effeminate laugh ...
the shadows.

old Spanish people who
knew him, stayed off the
road at night, told
these stories of a destroyed
world while all fell
around them.

small town. a happiness
for children in old stories,
dreaming guns & battles,
bullets that never hurt,
scalpings that somehow
left the hair intact.

homestead. its uncured
wood rotted in the earth
until at last it broke
of its own weight, split
exposing the stained years
of the living.

The Carpenter

odor of
tobacco—

latakia
perique
oil

(at some point
what surrounds
a man
becomes him

birds curl into form
the sharp air
is bright

with their woodchip smell

my granduncle
his long hands stroke
a hurtling plane
& dreams
shape themselves
from fragrant wood—

cedar
oak
rich walnut

his hands, knobbed & grained
make cabinets rise,
gleam in the oiled light

The Carpenter's Wife: Rose

who, as a young girl,
hid in a wrinkled skin.

I saw her peeping out
of dry blue eyes, caught
a scent of lavender sachet,
dusty lace: her true ways
hidden behind gold glasses.

in her hands she remained
swift, gentle.

sadness surrounds her,
leaves that, as years,
curled, fell gracefully
curved past shyness &
her youth shone out in flowers
in songs hummed while her
stiff hands repaired
the wreckage brought daily
to her house, turning
in dust, spun past memories:

her lithe eyes take
in love a form
both comely & caressed

—as a singing bird, she arises,
walks, aged bones left easily behind.

The Sea

*On the beach
the ocean ends in water.*

—George Oppen
The Materials

The crisp line, taut, in all
intimations, thrown out, cork circling
the water, splash, my hand

reaching out

—the call, rightly named, these
Materials, the call is there
simple, demanding

response and a certain
attention to pulse, the
movement of whatever the work

asks of a man—is that what
I'm trying to say, a man,
and how, sometimes, he doesn't

drown. Coming up spitting
salt water, safely past the
screws, it *is* a man
intact who waves

from the calm wake; behind
him the sea clear, oceans
held in place by a line.

The Juggler

(After Richard Wilbur & Andre Gide

sirventes

three crimson balls
catching the fire
the crimson, slipping

sun, he, juggler
fingertips jabbing
the balls hurtling

in his determined
already proscribed
orbits. planets.

Hands stop. geometric
perfection, universe
falls, the fool runs

away laughing, bells
bouncing copper lights,
his the motley, us, fools

more fools for wanting
more show, after all
he gave illusion,

Fools, good gods made
them wise enough for
games. three broken

globes for us, don't
pick them up don't
mind, it's a game.

Roualt: "A Clown"

whose face hangs
down

    skull
showing through.

a copy. artfully
made, catching the light
brushstrokes, the pigment's
texture.

it was sold
for its frame two
-fifty, the old man
said, I'll give you
the picture

his own face
redveined, stetson
hat cocked to one side
ridges of the eye sockets
cheekbones showing through
a little.

Day of the Pig

—Sacramento Mountains, 1940

one of them, grazing the still
meadow, slightly behind the others.
a man in our hunting party who wished
despite warnings "to have fresh pig
for supper"

    spotted domestics
gone wild, they were taller, heavier
than javelinas, meaner
my father said

    be ready to run
but there wasn't time, the fool
missed & the pregnant young sow, black spotted
white in the early dusk, charged
faster than I ever knew a pig could run,
low, the pounding of her sharp hooves

    & I dropped to one knee, opened
fire: saw dust fly from .22 hits,
head on, pig coming, dust,
an angry snapping of teeth

until his 30/30 slug caught her flush
& spun her down, blood trickling
from her relaxing snout

we cut her open, keeping an eye
to the rest of the sounder, dressed
her & later, beside a mesquite wood fire
the man ate shining piglets
one after the other, saying
how delicious they were, smacked
his lips and laughed, sun already
down—a clear moon lighting
the still mesa.

Sounds, Deafening from Battle

(for D.H. who once asked how
it felt

Sounds, deafening from battle,
these ears by concussion webbed
cracked into lattices are webs
supporting sound in a loose matrix.

Yet enough gets left for the polarities,
the relevances: without real distinction
the bullfrog still grunts differently
from the pig: the lowhunting owl
the diving hawk, screams of victim
mice & rabbits, are much the same.

The sounds brother one
another, even in damaged ears:
structures are structures, my friend;
all limits, limit equally and

a man who takes up a sword, as the Bible
would state it, expects to lose some
thing, a part, at the doing of it.

The battle I mean. The loss.
They are the payments or perhaps

only rewards. "A neat wound,"
prays the soldier, "that I might have

one to take me home." It is
con-sequence counts, after action.

Notes on Physical Structures

—for Drummond Hadley

i

deep silence.
a hollow existing, surrounded
by sound.

a structure.

content, measured by noise
the way clearings are measured
in part by enclosing trees.

a deep hole.

a well a boy shouted
down, years ago &
the echo keeps

circling: the center
of that echo, silence

& a sense of falling
falling right on through

a gateway stranger
even than night.

ii

three bells
ringing, a golden
clapper for each.

blonde curls, a small
girl, head caught in sun

measure me the aura

indicate beyond what
hue the radiance

becomes illusion: rising,
when she speaks, you

look at her lips but
the colors over-run their limits
& where does she begin
where, end?

* * *

three golden bells
& as Cummings said, the notes
buzz as bees

      —a sadness, this
walking blind when
worlds telescope into
one another, colors

radiating every
where the sun shines
with different
intent

      —this girl, she unfolds
      out of the sun

iii

in the dark (that
word again, unexplored

in defining
in letting the mind become
crystalline with light, a
structure beyond purpose
or proposing

—meditatively, probing

we come to
gray shapes, old deeds
forms taking senseless
patterns, acting out
pantomimes

      -clown
graces, ancient tricks
learned for children

& gibbered into night:
the dark (containing all
light has not touched

is not a question
but its own answer: what we
are, we think we are not.

it is the same with dark
only not so plain.

iv

A. $F = ma$

Force, as any good physicist knows
is equal to no thing
being instead some envelopment
some surge of particles
which perhaps is the dynamic
particle itself

One notes the wind
most when dust is carried or
its strength is felt but
where is wind-ness & who
has held the specimen gale
in a labeled bottle?

B. The Perspective: Narrowed Vision

that this, what one
sees is worth
the saying, one
must assume:

a girl skipping rope
in the dust

her bare feet
burnished to collages
of mica, she gets seen

best through
narrowed eyes, where
she appears

an agile flower
tall, flexible, gold
chrysanthemum

caught in wind
in color while
the sun, hung low,

is cut by the
thin moon of rope &
falls

... skipping girl
made momentarily bright
on a dry hillside

flashes of
various, particolored light:
youth, scattered in
dark leaves
at her feet.

v

as can be
seen, little
is known (most,
most of that

lies.

it's a question: which
reality do

you

accept? I'll take
that green one, that
blue one & just a slice of
purple, if you
please

—old worlds spin out above
  our heads, counting the brushed
  stars, flaming with

  forgotten light, they hide
  darker worlds

I would enter in
my finger, like Alice
into her Glass

or capture the universe
with the structure
of an eye, swirling

looking outward toward
bright clusters, Grails
of infinite changes,
startling firebursts:
behind flowers, a girl,
a sheen on her clear skin
changing, winks back
at me.

vi

for her
a little love song
to eternity:

a touch, something
to feel with

o, if I could sing!
I'd release the mountains
back to flame, the seas
would open, magnetic
flowers!

The Old Flyer

Double-spanning wings, biplane
struts & wires howling
out of the sun
diving

        &the marriage photograph:
        a slim young officer with
        wings, a silver blur on
        the old print.

            She, dark
        crazed eyes, off to one
        side, slightly cowering.

Darkness splits, the echoes
of machineguns behind, crosses
fall lazily
trailing flames

        She, running, screaming
        in the night, hides under
        her mother's bed, sobbing
        still in her bridal gown.

On the wall, a propeller.
German. Splintered at

one tip. Carefully
varnished, glistening.

      —What had they all to do, a Spad
        circling in high light, the
        guns & later, the handsome face
        (no death hides in the eyes of
         the photo, the bride
         never returns

What had any thing to do
with this fat old man behind
the beer, smiling into the
night, tapping his fingers?

Day of the Snake

My sister, 3 years old in a pinafore, sought
shade from our hard New Mexico sun, the white
blazes on the Hereford cattle at the line
camp, her under the one tree, beside the wind
mill

      —a rock beside her foot, out of
          shade grew into awareness,
          a prickle at the back ...
          hesitation

          the moving coils,
          dark tongue flicked
          in, back

an inch from her foot the rockflat head
steady eyes, her bare foot, vulnerability
of a baby before the sun

& how our father protested
when the rancher killed the heatpassive snake
—a 5 foot Diamondback, saying
with perfect truth, he spared
my daughter, god damn it let
him live

later, the snake's head crushed, spreading
to rock, rattles quivering musically
we walked away, blazing suns
about our heads.

Sleeping Baby

Beat your hard tight
little fists against
the air

the fight once begun
before whatever goal
is always there, the

dreams you dream as
vivid as those haunting
my head, listen,

we old ones roll & toss
our lives away while
who knows what you dream?

The old language fresh
on your lips, Atlantis
sings and ancient mountains

rise in memory: before
this safe bed seas rise up
sleep is a distant voyage
never to be taken, lightly.

The Politicians

                              come
come here with full bellies
& shined shoes to the one street
of San Miguel, talking, waving
hands, their harsh gringo Spanish
shouted in the hanging dust
of the square

        the men of the town
stand uneasy, aware of their hard
hands, the blue of the stranger's
eyes, their own mudcrusted boots
stiff with clay

they are ashamed these men
whose hands are strong with work & loving.
they listen. then go to the bar,
beer & red wine, jukebox Infante songs,
his dead voice singing of a Mexico
which was sad, beautiful, but theirs
—riding free across a green land,
gritos on their lips & dead politicians
fall, one-by-one before their dreaming guns.

A Birthday Poem for Diana Hadley

Being,
in the smaller senses
—flowers
girls

are distinctly touches,
movements within the air
perceiving, enveloping
them, what they are

IS

slender stalks, opening
blossoms

a green-ness
a texture the *eye*
takes on the way skin
accepts breezes
sharp points of branches

—as I said
the touches, some girls,
they brush like flowers
against men.

Note to a Sister

Blood is dark, heavy with
mossed memories. Relationship,
a treacherous tie, bound by
terrors of childhood, guilts
past the forgiving.

We pass, parallel showers of stars,
committed, grope toward absolution
in a world where each holds one
piece only of a crucial puzzle:

      mine,
    a jagged tear, a torment.
    endlessly I reach, retreat,
    lunging back & out
    —seeking to steal the peace
    that might be given, in love.

Playmate

And because
of him, the small box carried at shoulder
height, high school boys somber in
black and cracking no smiles missed
football practice, stood, the heavy
little box rubbing one shoulder, awkward,
bearing down

From the church—singing.
I pulled the collar of my peajacket tight,
I sat across the street in the cold winds
preceding Spring trying to imagine Charlie:
him letting anyone keep him in that satin box.
All that crying, and him hating roses, getting
dressed up when it wasn't even Sunday, lying
there, in that sissy box.

Firecrackers in June

all day the firing goes on:
bursts of flame after dark bright
fireflies of laughter, boys screaming
& the older people being tolerant,
uneasy

—they're illegal here
in San Miguel, must be brought
from Texas not far away in crisp
crinkling packages, faces of tigers
Black Cats, spitting

—how to tell
my son (who's 3) the dangers, the
quick fears caught in all that beauty
& noise? How to speak of real gun
fire, my nervousness when firecrackers
go off behind my back? In what world
do not these eyes, flared in heart
stopping excitement stir memories
sympathy? drums beating, quick
step march & armies sweep forward
out of a boy's blazing eyes.

The Name

I tried to call out
but shame was nothing
to talk about.

   strange
how warmly your eyes
became pain as you talked

placing your hands
upon his shoulders
as if they were birds

and I, too ashamed
to speak your name.

bloodtotem

the pig mask upon the wall
has carved eyes & a snout
ridged & grooved by knife

the pig mask upon the wall
has four eyes: two for it,
two for a man in looking through

to see the world in a charge,
grasses flashing by, in red eyes
inflamed to a boar's hatred

the pig mask upon the wall
is its own incantation, unleashes
tusked furies, old fears

of lunging, driving lusts
—blood & fighting, ripped
bellies, clicking teeth

& the sweet warmth of blood
trickling down the jowls: pig
mask, upon the wall. passive.

in tension. made of man the mask
startles the breathing, holds
in ceremonial wood the imaged

ancient king, killmaster
of the ages: with a warrior's cry
he bears the mask before him

a lens of gleaming wood
while out of darkness behind
comes a snuffling, & luminous eyes.

GRAVES REGISTRY

"Graves Registry":   A Joint Service Operation that comes in after
battles, & wars, to count the dead, identify bones,
draw up a total of what has been lost . . .

Aus dunklem Wein und Tausend Rosen rinnt die Stunde
rauschend in den Traum der Nacht.

(Note: All German epigraphs are to be found
in *The Lay of the Love & Death of Coronet*
Christopher Rilke by Rainer Maria Rilke.)

Part One: Korea—Japan, 1950–53

I

...*Wein, leuchtend*
in eisernen Hauben. Wein? Oder
Blut?—Wer kanns unterscheiden?

Some thing is coming.

a significance, growing, emerges
from the deep green water, slick
with oil. At first it shows a low shape,
resembles a shark, or a killer whale:

long & dark, with fins.

Nearer the surface, a glow of blue,
a gleam from the cockpit, sense
of someone within—a paleness
viewed through uncertain light.

The increasing apprehension, uneasy
excitement.

It's free. The cables of the straining crane
draw taut & the water opens, parts with suction
& gurgles

—the plane, wings shorn off, body
intact, is lifted, gleaming, blue,
paint freshly wet into the bright
sun of Tokyo Bay.

Pilot & gunner sit stiff
in their proper places; radioman
below, can't be seen, the awareness
of him alone is there

each has his goggles set, heads
leaning slightly forward against
the restraining straps. Lenses
wink dully.

Then in the vanishing water
in the bright air flesh slides off long dead
skulls, the helmets shrink & collapse
out of sight as the hook drops the TBM, looking
almost new, on the waiting barge.

NB: an autopsy revealed
the pilot was killed
by one piece of shrapnel
which neatly severed
each vertebra in turn.
the gunner & the radioman
were alive when the plane
hit the water.

II

"China Night"

I ain't got no
yo-o-yo
(from our sailors' version
of the original Japanese
lyrics)

night. fire in the *hibachi*
low, none of us speaking japanese &
that song playing somewhere in the distance
while we fumbled with girls who giggled
who were children when their men carried
that song through Manchuria, through
China & the Philippines.

           Now it becomes
our turn, girls soft & warm the *hibachi*
smoking & all youth to be served while
the song, their song, sounded again & again
through ricepaper halls, the growing darkness,
sleep silencing finally us all. Coals,
coals of the brief fire, old love song,
ghost voices, spinning on.

III

(R & R, Korea 1950)

on the beach party from the carrier
lying off Kwajalein, a haze of
bluegray smoke rising from her:

the men. drinking cheap shipboard
beer, forcing themselves to live
it high under the hot sun.

beyond them, the clean white
of the Shore Patrol. I,
their officer, hoping

for no trouble, know better
& watch one redhead run
crazy through a hammerlock
my SP has on him

see the fury in his face
dissolve to wonder & shock
as the pain of his shattered
elbow hits him

give the orders & watch them
carry him, fainting, to the boat
hospital bound

—walk on, poking into the brush, scaring
the *jo-ro* hill girls; & the men they drew

shuffle off, anger of gold braid
in their eyes.

there it is.

a rusted .45, clip in,
hammer back, safety off.
in its way, dangerous
as a handgrenade, there
since World War II.

I carry it uneasily, hiding
it from the men (who need more
attention now, beer hitting their
minds, breaking loose with whoops

see my SP's trying not to hurt
them, pity on their faces, a little
envy

giving orders, trying to get free
long enough to give that weapon
a decent burial.

IV

Und bebende Trommeln.

the captain:

Army of the United States. About 40,
small, lean. Colt .32 Auto

snug under his armpit, the kind eyes
of somebody's uncle.

His men: tall for Koreans, all
carried M-1's (because there, big men
have big rifles, it is the custom

& what happened to his eyes
the changes when he spoke of their raids
of villages flaming, women & children
machinegunned as they ran
screaming from their huts:

>   his own sense of the stillness
>   (which he told of) as the Gray
>   Marine engines caught & they
>   drew away, leaving the bodies
>   in their white clothes
>   sprawled here & there, big
>   & small, blood seeping into
>   white, junks slipping
>   smoothly away

V

. . . ganz in Waffen

Along the coast heavy clouds of dawn
bucked and heaved, arteries of flame pulsed
subsided

         aboard ship, signal flags
      popped in the wind
& slowly the amphibious squadron took station;
the flagship, dead center of the formation,
moved slowly, then faster

         quiet intensified.
      no one spoke, the ship scuttled
      its 11 knots across a passive sea

            Gunflashes grew vivid now
but still they heard only the engines of the ship,
the wind. A cruiser, lying off a small island
rocked, fired in heavy salvos

         their LST followed
      the breeze-whipped Flag
      straight for the beach
      & the guns . . .

He'd been watching his face,
speaking to him occasionally,
sensing the recruited strength.
The boy rarely answered.

The guns could be heard now. Low, distant.
Heavy 8″ whooms! lighter 5's, auto 3's
from the cruiser. A few destroyers also
popped away when suddenly a round from the beach
burst off the bow into a
yellow flower

the kid broke, no real danger
but he broke. It was in
his eyes, in terror
he edged for the hatch

The officer stopped him with his voice. Quick, flat.
The boy looked about ten standing there, the wind
from the open bridge tugging his hair.
Come back here, he said. The boy did.
Stand here by me, he ordered. He did, close.
They went through the action that way, & neither
was afraid.

VI

(Korea, 1952)

guerrilla camp

We arrived at Sok To
before dawn, caught the last
of the tide & slipped the LST's bow
high on the beach.

        he was waiting, bent
        slightly over, hiding
        his hand. he didn't
        wave.

Later, after a good breakfast
aboard, an Army captain took
us on a tour of the guerrilla
camp:

        & he followed, tagged
        along like somebody's
        dog. a tall Korean,
        patient.

We were shown the kitchens, & the
tent barracks, the specially built
junks with their concealed engines

        & he watched, never
        leaving us with his
        eyes

Through the hospital, saw four
sheetcovered bodies from the
raid the night before, didn't
ask whose men they were, spoke
kindly to the wounded & gave
them cigarettes

        until he strode up,
        stuck his shattered hand
        in my face, anger & hatred
        flaming in his eyes &
        shouted & shouted & shouted

        waving that hand, the
        bones crumpled by

a rifle slug & pushed
almost through the skin,
hardened into a glistening
knot

He was one of ours, a retired fighter,
about my age, my height. They told me
he wanted to know how a man
could farm
with a hand like that.

VII

the singer

who did sing, whose voice
spoke out of a guitar's darkness;
in a clear young night he
sang midwatches away, telling
of country lands, of growing crops
green corn, tall in the fields
of Kentucky; dark songs of loves,
concerns and ancient questions
he had not yet lived to confirm
or deny.

17. About 6'1". Heavyset,
with plowman's hands & walk.

Then there was my gun.
In its way, it sang too. Clean machine
oiled & perfect, the slide flashed
back over my relaxed hand pow. pow. pow.
& .45 wadcutter slugs crimped neat holes
in the fluttering paper; the gun
was a happiness to my hand.

Many nights that boy was the whole
watch as I would lean against the flying
bridge, coffee growing cold in my cup,
listening to that voice singing out
the darkness ahead.

Then came the time in port. Just before
the invasion. The gunner's mates were
cleaning all weapons for the coming action &
claimed mine too.

I was on the bridge
checking the charts. An indistinct
popping sound. Silence.
Running feet, & shouts.

When I got back to the fantail
he was lying there, his boy's face
twisted & gray, big farmer's hands
held in his guts, guitar beside him.

My gun in the destroyed gunner mate's hand.
Smoking faintly.
These are the things that get lost.
Guitars. Guns. Hands to hold
onto them.

VIII

—U.S.S. *Valley Forge,* 1950

The Circle

Out of the stirrings of the Yellow Sea,
20 miles off from Inchon Channel
we came to—blue leis
thrown on the water.

Sea, glassy. no wind.
I sat atop a 5″ director, the ship
steamed on, no planes in sight:
a pleasant gunwatch, little excitement,
lost in quiet.

The first I knew we
were among them, circles of men
bound in faded blue lifejackets,
lashed together

Most of the men leaned
back, heads bobbing against
kapok collars, mouths open,
tongues swollen

—hundreds of them.
We steamed by, group after group,
for all my watch. I searched for

any sign of motion, any gesture
of any hand, but soon I just
watched as

   bobbing gently, each circle
   undulated, moved independently;
   once or twice a hand did flop
   & I caught the man's face in
   my binoculars instantly,
   slowly let them drop

We sailed on. I suppose that's all
there is to say: wartime commitments,
the necessity for being where you must
be & when

   they were dead, hundreds
of them, a troopship gone down somewhere
—Korean, uncounted.

   I remember one man, remember
   him clearly. God knows why
   but his ass was up instead
   of his head; no pants left,
   his buttocks glistened
   grayish white in the clear sun.
   the only one.

& we steamed on, routine patrol,
launched planes at 1800 for night

CAP, leaving the last of the circles
rocking gently in our darkening wake.

> *. . . seid stolz: Ich trage die Fahne,*
> *seid ohne Sorge: Ich trage die Fahne,*
> *habt mich lieb: Ich trage die Fahne—*

> *   *   *

> *. . . und die reglose Fahne hat unruhige*
> *Schatten. Sie träumt.*

IX

high noon

little Korean village, by the
Yellow Sea, full of drying squid,
kids, the people follow with
hunger in their eyes

> *three officers, spitclean*
> *in pressed khakis, warm parkas*
> *to take the bite off the springtime*
> *cold, out walking seeing the sights—*

Only one was armed. A Colt snuggled in smooth
leather, slapping the outer thigh, loaded
but no round in chamber, flap of the holster
closed.

a gun has a speaking voice, did
you know that? a quiet
certainty looking out of the muzzle
& then it speaks

A gun at the side, always a concern: a charged
field, a potential, like the sex between a man's
legs.

Three officers out walking the sun,
easy, safe as only Americans (or Romans,
long ago) can be safe, untouched by hunger,
eyes seeing sights, quaint brushes with
unreal picturepostcard suffering, out
walking

& suddenly. the street.
lined with thin watchful men.
silent. eyes upon them, the
hatred, passive

The young officer, hand drawn halfway down
to the living gun, stopped. The motion was
enough. Men stirred, then froze—a new
possibility intruded; they watched the hand,
cocked, ready—in fear—to strike.

slowly they walked, no
retreat, down every footstep
of the street, eyes upon
them, the bright yellow openings
in the buildings ahead drew
them, hungering

63

That they made it is no concern, that
they turned into sunlight, free, muscles
of shoulders relaxing, sudden laughs
Nor is it any more important
what the Army major said:

they were lucky, two sailors
had been cut down on that very street
the week before. "Kill-or-Capture" teams
operating from North Korea, they'd
even gotten two officers on the steps of
headquarters in Seoul, he said.

Somehow all that was known, understood.
The gun, it knew, the cocked hand
knew

What remained was the gun, the
walk, cold Spring sun, gleaming
eyes. the test. again, those
things get lost, drive on out of
the blood when least expected: bright

> *bright flashes, sense of*
> *the cocked hand, expectant*
> *in the swirling world*
> *of combat. a surety of steel.*
> *calm hands.*

X

"Bist Du die Nacht?"

the girl,

in an Inchon officers club,
small breasts, thin indirect face
but with a silk gown, marks of rank
about her

      & how easily she came
later, in the dark, the lips parted
Korean words in passion in light
not understood

      the crinkle of paper,
passing hands

XI

guns

chattering guns, bright flames
about their mouths, talking an old
tongue through

     their beauty gets forgotten

the quick rush of a kind of singing
moving toward to gunfire to death which
asks nothing but fearlessness
crazy shouts

dying men, in their breathing,
to leave curious legends
terror
pieces of rusted metal

XII

body at sea

back home. The States.
operational cruise, to keep
the hand in. Sailors grow
old away from sea the
Commodore said, laughing

       —steaming along
California coast, hard
beautiful strong tides
catching the rudder, currents
themselves

The Quartermaster of the Watch
spotted him. Called the OOD.
"Sir, there's something out there."

              too far away
          only a bit of darker blue, strangely
          formed log, debris

the stomach knew.

"Left Standard Rudder! Corpsman
to the Bridge!"

By the time the engines stopped
the deck was lined by crew, men

coming up from the hatches, the
swiftness of the word, spreading:

      everybody watched.
      Mac slipped the wire stretcher
      under the floating body, his
      face in the boat revealed
      —before the stench hit—
      how long the sea held this man.

"Raise Away!" the men hit the line
smoothly & the stretcher turned
slowly as it rose. The men, silent.
Just at deck level, it swung,
the man, on his belly, dressed in
blue denim, arms crumpled beneath
him

              dead milky wideopen
              eyes
              the crabtorn face

—dark gulls, to mark that day, a memory
of war, going on, on, man-to-sea, man-to-man,
the sounded, plumbed war rose up, giant breakers
deafening beaches ahead.

XIII

waterfront bars

& how they look—from the sea
the neon glitter softens, grows
warm

    —a man can almost smell
beer, women

From Beppu, on the Inland Sea,
the giant "Asahi" beersign stood
steady as any navigational light

        drew, caught
attention: we, sailing by
returned to seadamp bunks
strong coffee

3 months of service duty ahead
north of the bombline &
then back we came, wondering

    —lights of Yokusuka, Sasebo,
Yokohama. We sailed to them
each in turn. Worlds brushed,
passed

      each in turn.

—leaving the darkness of night
watches, silver turning of screws,
wake piled high behind
the blackened ship: little pieces
of a man, left here, there.

XIV

sea songs for women

"To Those We Leave Behind"
—Old Navy Toast

such power, recorded, is the trace
of days, bright promises of what
could have been

dreams
dreams of young blood, girls
shining & clean in the sunshine
of springtime beaches

crinkling hair & the endless, forever
repeated words, out of a common pulse,
speaking of the love's concerns:

bright moon, rising
as it did, over Sumeria,
over Mu, over the cracked
terraces of drowned Atlantis

—Sisters, companions, died in
locked arms, time time again

turned upon the words spoken
half-remembered, memory of the
pale lady rising out of foam

gesturing, the clean
drive of cycles turning

love, speaking like guitars
a singing that drives the night
around us like a robe.

XV

the mistress

and there was Akiko.
her child's face, her hatred
of all Americans, save one:

whom he held in his arms,
Akiko. vision of a dead brother
blown to pieces in front of her
his brains on her dress.

he, four. she, ten.

Akiko, who was ashamed
not of loving but of
forgetting

while his own dead
floated the Yellow Sea
burned slowly in planes
died gasping, jagged holes
in their chests

they held each other
through horrors higher
than language, built

a brightness to curtain
the blue, newly made cannon
nightmare bombs stamped "U.S.A."

Und da schämt er sich fur sein weisses Kleid.
Und mochte weit und allein und in Waffen sein.
Ganz in Waffen.

XVI

December, 1952

Back to the combat zone.

Ships, exactly stationed, at darkness
their wakes catch white fire, long graceful lines
blue stacksmoke, fading to night

red battle lamps, men walking
ghosts in the chain lockers

old chanties sung in the small watches
of morning

Nelson, battle signals snapping,
coming about, broadside ready

Farragut, headed in . . .
the shores blazing with light
exploding shells a terror,
the calm voice on the bridge

Skeleton crews, prize ships,
returning to Ur of the Chaldees, swords raised
gleaming before the dying sun

A blue United Nations patch on the arm, a new
dream. One World. One
Nation.

Peace.

The old bangles, dangled
once more, always working,
buying allegiances

                  stabbing
              tracers hit a village,
              the screams of women, children
              men die

It is when the bodies are counted
man sees the cost of lies, tricks

that blind the eyes of the young. *Freedom.*
Death. *A life safe for.* The Dead.

Casualties are statistics
for a rising New York Stock Market—
its ticker tapes hail the darkeyed
survivors, and cash registers
click, all over the nation, these men
deceive themselves. War is for. The Dead.

XVII

The Flag

barred with blood,
blue of virgins, all
of them, Aztec Corn Mother,
ancient Lady of the Earth,
Holy Woman

White, with the color
of purity

a piece of cloth
tattering in the Eastern wind

XVIII

combat mission

In the Korean night they drank
12-year-old Scotch, talked warm

around the oilcan stove, their holstered
.45's dragging the earthen floor as
they squatted, glow of liquor creeping
home inside the parkas, old stove
sucking at the night's cold air

—in a ruined merchant's house
pocked with rounds from invasion
they rebuilt against the night:
2 Navy officers, 1 Marine from the line,
10 miles away, lifted their cups against
the darkness, the rumbles rolling forward.

While fires flickered on the hills
they went, confident, out into a night
where heavy weapons grumbled
& a Korean boy played "China Night"
on a squeaky phonograph, dreaming,
as they were, of brown women,
of any warm bed before gunfire,
the greater dream of battle.

XIX

Cargo

Sailing on, orders for Sok To, north
of the bombline. Our LST loaded gunnel
to gunnel with high-octane gas, ammo

> "A gook with a .45
> could sink us," a boatswain

mate says, glancing down
at the darkening water

Headed in, through the slim channels
islands blackening to either side,
the shore batteries unseen but sensed
nothing to shoot back with

                              a bomb,
a torpedo—Long Slow Target, with
orders.

About midnight, reading a chart
by masked flashlight, speaking in whispers,
though the engines are loud in our ears,
steaming through the tightest passage,
Communist shore to starboard, our island
to port when

                    heavy shore rifles cut loose
                    shells whirr overhead, the young
                    helmsman ducks, is straightened
                    by a snapped order

                    & the island explodes
                    blazing gasoline
                    bursting munitions

then U.S. jet engines swoosh & napalm douses
the shore batteries in standing waves of fire—

somehow the screams, the dying got lost

the chart is brilliant in light
we sail on, walls of red
to either side the dying
fight back

we, steaming on,
carrying our own deaths
deep in our bellies.

XX

hiroshima. hiro-
shima. hi-ro-shi-ma.

I, an American, try
to say that word, to
pronounce it like
my Japanese girl, turning
my tongue on it
as its own streets
turned & twisted,
radiating outward

—to speak, through
this sign, what
it is to be american,
japanese in a century
of terror

my face it
shapes itself to tongue;

her eyes gleam back, mirrored,
I speak the word & see
—oval eyes, a burned cheek,
trace the scars
with shaking fingers

XXI

commentary

After the raid, the bodies
are lined on the beach. We can
see them across the way, the living
standing beside them in their white
robes, the wind hitting in gusts
across the separating bay

that these men died
that our guerrillas shot them
down in a darkness
is perhaps not so important.

God kills, they say
justifying man's ways
to those patterns they
see surround them

deaths. lists of victims
in a language the uncle
back home couldn't read
if he saw it, whose enemies

are always faceless, numbers
in a paper blowing in the
Stateside wind.

How many bodies would
fill a room
living room with TV, soft
chairs & the hiss
of opened beer?

We have killed more.
The children's bodies alone,
would suffice.

The women, their admittedly
brown faces frozen in the agony
of steel buried in their stomachs,
they too would be enough

but aren't, are
finally not piled high enough
the cost of war must be paid, bullets
made for firing, fired. O
do not dream of peace while such bodies
line the beaches & dead men float
the seas, waving, their hands
beckoning
                rot, white bones
          settle on yellow bottom mud.

XXII

truce

Now the pace changes.
Ships come home, cruisers
their stacks still, blow
no more blue trails over the sea . . .

Truce.

& no more green
wakes, swirling white
bubbles shining
blades, turning

Uniforms in mothballs,
gold braid tarnishing,
ribbons stuck with stars,
faded emblems.

The Flag, dreams.

Factories, burning
with orange smoke, cut
steel plates with blue
arcs, welders patch up
the weapons
of war

dream.

. . . und die sechzehn runden Säbel,
die auf ihn zuspringen, Strahl um
                                 Strahl,
sind ein Fest.
Eine lachende Wasserkunst.

Part Two: Seascapes

the ex-officer, navy

the man, in whose eyes gunfire
is a memory, a restless dream
of stuttering mouths, bright flame

a man, who no matter how long the days
faces still the combat, the long night's terror—

> beyond the shoreline, gray muzzles train,
> the destroyer's bow breaks cleanly, all mounts
> at ready, general quarters: racing feet
> grunting rasping horn. tight stomach.
> knotted muscles in the shoulder, neck.

on white bare feet, with flaring eyes he greets
the morning, peace—advancing age. the dead faces once
again firm, smiling, ready for battle fade
gray smoke against a city's sun.

The Bridge, the Sea

At night, the LST bucking low waves
moon ten degrees on the port quarter, a following
wind and the crew sleeping below.

> The open bridge
overhangs the sea, waves slapping bow, the engines
vibrate, tickle, reassure the palm of the resting hand.

Of all watches, the mid is longest. OOD's love it
fear it: in those grave endings of the night the sea
is spokesman, a gay killer who must be watched
because of his charms . . .

sea, sea gods dancing
in the green, green eye . . . the crew sleeps on
below, engines push a phosphorescent wake
into darkness.

Magic

3, 4, 5,
learning to count:
9, 10, 11.
4 ways into your
heart I 3 speak 5
charms against the
drift of 9 tides 4
moons 5 yellow roses;
learning to count: the
1, 2, 3, 4, the how many
determined by a look
in your 2 eyes, the night
5, 5! & what we can do.
What we
            can
                    DO.

The Sailor Come Home

I,
driven halfmad.

The eyes of my children
confront me, their father
—in his madness, to speak
not of the love borne
them but in airs of
old seatunes, chanties,
anchor-hauls, rope-pulls,
Erie canal songs, all
mad. My children have
dark eyes and are terrible
with innocence.

The Hanging of Billy Budd

the quick
—jerk

i

what would a man
see if his eyes
were not blindfold?

the stretching sea?

a wake bubbling
blue, behind the gulls
a darkness?

a young face
halfshut eyes
looking out

what would they
see?

ii

an innocence

    (no thing
  stands as innocent as the
sea, knowing no
  ·wrongs, a simple
     power

in one man
the flash of a knife
awakens, dark thunders

all men perhaps facing the
same in this fierce
excitement

and at a man's
own death?

a rough tickle
about the neck, wind
kicking at the hair
high above, looking
down

what would he see
but the easy pitching
ship, the pale faces
the watch, assembled
below

an innocent sea
calm as God's eyes

The Seaman

Near the seashore's changing arc, sands
slip back, tides push against the
land a bobbing shape, bluedenimed shoulders
humped, derelict, laced with foam, his face
pounds on bottom coral

     —eyes of coral, webbed
& split by salt he arrives messenger
of no known ship, a calling
left before sea

    Above sirens
thudding bare feet rush to rescue
what cannot be saved, the sea's low rolls
lift the husky body, the pale hands push
against the sand & the chipped, the wrinkled
eyes, head rising, the eyes of a sailor
look last to the landbound men

& I
who no longer go to sea,

turn away, turn
away, the sounds of sea
at my back, turn, turn
away.

Part III: New Moon, Inland Sea

—for George & Angie

i

—that this one dreamed ship still
cuts her way, sea

foam, that at night a landbound bed
breaks & rolls:
shore bedroom smelling of new paint

salt
trace of kelp

memories of:

a new moon just arcing the porthole's circle
the anticipation of cruising
of clanking, of heaving twisting
anchorchain turning up

bubbles
of yellow mud

ii

slowly, the screws turn
the green wake carries

                charged water,
                  white, touches
                    of blue

        the heavy shudder of engines
               stuttering tinkle
                    of the engineorder

        telegraph and the landbound body
                    relives the feel:

                        cold brass, a turk's head
                           at the spoke
                             of the helmsman's wheel

                Captain on the bridge,
          bosunpipes, a fair wind for the East

                      —coffee, in a chipped mug
                          steaming

                              then they

        the memories

        go under, the touches, skin
                    of the hand

iii

little ships, toy boats
        headed out; from
                Diamondhead the harbor

is a blue tub, winds catching
                scents, nets spreading

the brown skin of a diving girl
                is a kind of warcry

for the stiff white man, crisp navy jacket
gold buttons
                reflecting the sun, breeze
strong for Midway and in the mind,

                the passage, knived coral channels, holy
                blue water, pale jellyfish climb

                fall

                        —the oilslicked water

marking the ports as clearly as

                seagulls or

                        the black fins
                        departing sharks

iv

behind the wake, a sense of
what is left behind, watches that
through nights caught in
the tangible
                    brought awareness, senses
of not being alone, the sea
carrying with it the presence of wind
                    cargoes
                    of small lights

                —shining eyes before the ship
                    the bow breaks cleanly
                            through

        it is port
            that is dream

v

                        that is dreamed

that leapt before my eyes, that was sea.

sounds of ship, remembrances of
                    wind, stars
through the sextant, tiny flashes
to be fixed on charts with a sharp pencil,
points, lines crossed to make position

                    where none was before

—cigar smoke flying
       blue past the Quartermaster's
     ear

vi

       —for Drummy

Sail, Steam, Diesel, Ports-of-
Call, heavy with the fragrance of inland flowers
the husky cries of seabirds, splashes!
       of diving fisherhawks

    men-o-war, floating blobs
      in the stink of harbor life

fishing boats, headed out as you
    sail in, the lights
    along the shore, gleaming & warm

      —the one last voyage, then
that never is final; sailors fight off age
   lie for papers
     catch ships headed out again
      for deep water, the crisp
       breeze to freshen the nose

        beat the skin clean
        with salt

vii

Kobe. Yokosuka. Queen's Ferry. Portsmouth.
          Gloucester. Sea chanties heard in the night over
               the squalling of a steel ship
                    hard hit by sea

                         —underway, beating
          course out to the next port

                    which is always Paradise

                         —feeling the living ship
          spring out of the inbound tide,

               a dancer, catch current
               the beat: then to steam
                    tides bubbling behind

                         clear water ahead

viii

it is a sailor's dream. Nightmares come from tight
inland waters, channels, the one buoy's light
     that went out, bell that stopped ringing

a man's hard flat stomach leaning against
               his binoculars, them pressing
               against his solar plexus
                    the combing, open bridge

dreaming

an image before sea
of unmarked rocks, charts
that lie, currents drifting
too fast, too fast

it is a sailor's dream of sea

after, beyond fireplaces, in the peace
of inland homes. old prints of
ships beating around the Horn. ships,
and a globe, set spinning
by a restless finger:

clipper, sail full, running
free, nightbreeze at the nape
of the neck

moonlight a path through blue—
for the sailor in a man, remembrance
is a gleaming wake seen through
turning screws.

The Lion's Gate

To have met you there,
no lion either of us. Too much

fear.

          Too much pretense.

Wait.   You said.
And there I was, old enough, knowing
only the incidentals of life
open gates, that

               Out of the fires
around lion's mouths, the bright spires are
teeth which tear & rip—time, time proves
too merciless for me to wait
past the night time calling

—passing, as all things lovely, loving
          March winds, calling—
               Friend

without commitment, a touch of
skin against skin, eyes
that don't look away (the other's shame

becoming, finally, one's own culpability);
friend, without graces, and a few lies
proximity poses nothing.

                    Two granite lions
snarling at the night, that's us:
nothing between our teeth
but the night's lonely air.